Soul Whisperer

RELEASING LOST SOULS

ANNETTE RUGOLO

BALBOA.
PRESS

A DIVISION OF HAY HOUSE

Balboa Press books may be ordered through booksellers or by contacting:

Balboa Press
A Division of Hay House
1663 Liberty Drive
Bloomington, IN 47403
www.balboapress.com
1 (877) 407-4847

Print information available on the last page.

ISBN: 978-1-9822-0057-2 (sc)
ISBN: 978-1-9822-0059-6 (hc)
ISBN: 978-1-9822-0058-9 (e)

Library of Congress Control Number: 2018903391

Balboa Press rev. date: 04/24/2018

This book is dedicated to all of the lost souls
waiting for our help
to continue their journey home.

CONTENTS

PART ONE

PART TWO

ACKNOWLEDGEMENTS

There are two people I would like to thank who, without their help, this book would not have been written.

To Marie Diamond, my spiritual teacher, mentor, friend, and business partner who saw something in me that I could not see for myself. Thank you for holding a vision of my purpose in the world until I was ready to see for myself. You have opened me to possibilities and potential I could not have imagined. The transformation and expansion that has happened to me in this lifetime could not have occurred without you. To my friend and soul sister, I am truly grateful.

To Robin Mayfield, my editor. Thank you for entering my life when I needed you. You recognized something in the first version of this book and gently guided me to see the nugget within. Your expertise, keen eye and excitement for this book were instrumental in shaping it into something I am proud and honored to be presenting to the world.

Thanks also to my daughter, Angela Jones, for your illustrations and for continuing to help our family remember our connection to the creative arts.

Thank you to my husband, Tony Moch, for helping me stay grounded and for bringing fun and laughter into my life. You held a beautiful space for me during the process of creating this book.

And, finally, thank you to all of the souls, both incarnated and out of a body, who have been my teachers. I am honored to be sharing your message of healing with the world.

FOREWORD

There are times when I meet someone new and immediately recognize something very special about their energy field. This was the case with Annette Rugolo.

I first met Annette when she attended one of my classes in California. As a transformation teacher, I have taught many students over the years with the desire for each to connect and express their soul purpose in this lifetime. As the weekend class progressed, I sensed Annette was here to help others in a big wway.

It was wonderful to see her expand with each class she attended and I was happy when she stepped forward to begin teaching my methods. She accepted the position of Vice-President of Marie Diamond Global in 2007 and we worked together for five years, during which she supported my vision while expanding her own unique soul purpose.

As her spiritual growth continued, she became a Master Teacher of my Inner Diamond and Diamond Dowsing methods. She also created her own business of overseeing the distribution of Diamond products worldwide, in addition to offering her own unique brand of services.

Her transformation has taken her from a massage practice in Jamestown, North Dakota to being a global teacher, speaker and now author.

It has been with great joy to have my soul sister, Annette, share the vision to enlighten millions worldwide. I know this book was written with the purpose of bringing more light into people's lives and to support this vision.

– Marie Diamond

PREFACE

We all have moments that shape, adjust and change our perspective of the world in which we live. There are some moments, however, that transform our reality in ways that continue to reverberate throughout our lives.

It is always easy to remember these instances because they set us on a different path from where we were. Sometimes, only in hindsight, do we recognize the incredible shift they created in our lives.

There were three such moments in my life that helped shaped what I share in this book.

The first happened in the early 1990's while listening to a radio program. Someone was sharing a story about the parents of a four-year-old girl and their discovery of her very recent past life. At the time, I had no strong beliefs in regards to past lives. Having been raised in a Catholic family, we were taught that this life was our only lifetime, but I was a bit ambivalent about the concept.

The story was about a little girl who lived with her parents on the east coast of the United States. Sometime around the age of four, this little girl began talking in her sleep. As her parents checked in on her, they realized she was speaking French. This was really perplexing, as their daughter was never exposed to this language.

After a few nights of continued sleep talking, they made a recording and brought it to an interpreter. The parents were informed that their daughter was talking to people from a small village in France.

The parents, after finding that this village did exist, took a trip with their daughter and the interpreter, to further investigate.

As soon as they entered the village, their daughter became very excited and took them to all the places she knew from her previous lifetime. She remembered where she lived, where her friends and relatives lived, along with grocery stores, schools and more. She was able to tell them her name, along with the names of people she knew. All of the information was confirmed when they searched the town's records.

I was glued to the radio through the conclusion of this story. It was a moment in time when something I had sensed became reality. I knew without a doubt that past lives do exist.

The second moment came when I read about an experiment done sometime in the 1970's by a group of graduate students at Harvard.

For the study, they set up a fish tank and placed a piece of clear glass down the middle. They filled half of the tank with fish, leaving the other side empty. The fish lived in this world for several months until one day the glass was removed from the center of the tank.

What the students discovered through this experiment was that the fish did not swim to the other side and remained in their imaginary boundary.

Reading about this experiment created a profound shift in me. I immediately compared the fish in the tank to my own life and wondered what kinds of boundaries I grew up with that prevented me from experiencing life in a bigger way. It was at that moment that I committed to seeing life beyond the reality created by others.

The third moment came when I attended a meditation course created by Marie Diamond. Throughout the weekend, I felt I was being guided to the other side of the "fish tank." As I learned how to consciously connect to higher levels of consciousness within me, I literally felt my energy field expand.

The weekend had a profound effect on me. It was the doorway

that led me to my life's purpose of being a catalyst for healing and expanding consciousness in others.

I know that I could not have written this book without experiencing these three profound events.

We live in a multi-dimensional universe. The more you can open yourself to other worlds from a place of openness, the more you will learn that there is a multitude of beings that exist around us.

Much of what I share in this book comes from my own experience with spirits, the people who have called on me for help, and the spirits themselves.

You may have some awakened memories as you read this book. Pay attention to any sensations, dreams or feelings that may surface. I encourage you to trust the awakening that happens.

I invite you now into the world of earthbound and wandering spirits. I am excited and honored to be your guide.

Helping spirits advance in their evolution has been one of my greatest joys.

PART

One

Chapter One

HELP! THERE'S A SPIRIT IN MY HOUSE!

I had just purchased my own home in Fargo, North Dakota. The house was built in 1941 and was previously owned by just one couple the entire time. They were childless and had died 3 months apart from each other. Both were in their eighties when they died.

When I first looked at the house before buying, it was very dark. Heavy curtains covered the windows, the décor hearkened back to the 1960's and 25-watt light bulbs kept it dimly lit.

When getting to know my new neighbors, I was told that the husband was a successful businessman and very thrifty, not wasting any money on non-essentials such as extra lighting. His wife had never worked and spent most of her time in the house. She had been an alcoholic for many years.

The house was well constructed and aside from some cosmetic changes, had turned out to be a great find. I was happy with my new purchase and began immediately updating it and making it my own. New light fixtures, a coat of paint and a hardwood floor totally changed the look and feel of the house. I loved it.

After living there for about eighteen months, I had the

unexpected experience of meeting the former owner. It happened one night as I was drifting off to sleep.

Have you ever experienced the space between wake and sleep? It is something that feels so real and at the same time outside of what is considered reality. I was in this space the night I met her. I "saw" an elderly woman enter my bedroom. She started moving towards my husband but then saw that I was awake, changed her mind and began slowing coming to my side of the bed.

I was frozen in that moment, not being able to move or talk. She walked towards me with her right hand out in front of her and her index finger preparing to check me out.

I continued to stay frozen until she actually touched my arm, which triggered a blood-curdling scream, waking my husband and most likely the neighbors, too.

As I screamed, she disappeared into thin air and was gone. I never saw her again while I lived there but everyone who visited knew she hung out in the basement. Whenever my family came to visit, they felt very uncomfortable going down there, making only quick trips when absolutely necessary.

At the time, I did not have the information and the tools I now have that would have helped her. I also didn't understand much about spirits and why they continue to stay around after they pass. I had a lot to learn.

Having the tools to help spirits takes us from a place of powerlessness to a place of empowerment

Chapter Two

MY BROTHER'S SPIRIT

Sometimes a spirit attaches to a person, not through emotional trauma, but instead with hopes of clearing karma before they leave this dimension.

I had a personal experience with this after my brother died in 1989.

My brother was only thirty-eight years old when he died. I was living in Fargo and traveled to Milwaukee for the funeral. A few days later I returned to work and as I was sitting at my desk, I felt my brother's presence and assumed he came for a visit before his spirit moved on. I didn't know at the time that the soul of someone could attach to someone else's energy field after they passed.

Fast forward to 2005. I had been teaching meditation classes and had a deeper understanding of karma and how to release it. I was also doing a lot of work on myself and had become aware of some karmic energy with my dad.

There wasn't anything in particular happening at the time, except for the fact that, up until this point, I felt like I never had a very good relationship with him. When I called to visit (my parents lived out of state) and dad would answer, we would talk for a minute or two and he would pass the phone onto my mother.

I know a lot of dads are like this, but I felt there was something else there that I couldn't put my finger on.

During one of my exchanges with Marie Diamond, I was informed that my brother was still with me. I was told that his spirit stayed with me after he died as he felt I had the best chance of clearing the karma that we shared with our father.

I was shocked! Souls can connect with us after they die? My brother has been with me since 1989? How did he know I was going to be on this path?

I had so many questions!

But first, I needed to see and heal the relationship with my dad.

It turned out that my brother, my sister and I incarnated together to clear a karmic lifetime with our dad. In a previous lifetime, he was a Roman soldier and my siblings and I were part of a religious community that was persecuted.

The lifetime made sense when I looked at our childhood in this life. That same feeling of being punished was something we all lived in fear of. It affected each one of us in different ways.

The process of releasing a karmic lifetime means forgiving the soul who persecuted us or killed us in a past lifetime. Sometimes we have to forgive someone else. And sometimes we have to forgive ourselves.

I was very ready to release the karma that had hung over our heads since childhood and as I consciously forgave my dad, the soul of my brother was released. He was now free of the karma, as well.

Whenever a karmic lifetime is cleared, some kind of confirmation is received to verify that transformation of energy has occurred.

This happened in spades over the next few weeks.

The first thing that occurred was the phone call I made to my parent's home a few days after the clearing. My dad answered as usual but he couldn't pass the phone to my mom because she wasn't home.

What happened next astounded me. Instead of my dad cutting the conversation short, we ended up on the phone for almost an hour! This was the longest conversation I had ever had with my dad in my entire life! It was a warm, sweet connection I had not felt before that day. I was 53 years old and experienced a feeling of closeness with my dad that I had longed for my entire life.

As we said goodbye, he told me he loved me. I hung up the phone and tears of joy flowed. My relationship with my dad has continued to be filled with warmth. As I write this book, he is 87-years old and I am so happy to have had these years knowing him without any karmic energy interfering with our relationship.

The second thing that happened to confirm that the karma had cleared was a lucid dream I had about two weeks afterwards.

In the dream, my brother, sister and I were all on a stage singing "On Eagles Wings," a song I had sung with a few others at my brother's funeral. In the dream, a choir took over as we came to the chorus. At that moment, my brother and I turned to each other and gave each other a big hug. I woke up with the very real feeling of hugging my brother and again I cried out of pure joy.

The last confirmation I received came from my niece, my brother's oldest daughter. My two nieces were twelve and thirteen when my brother died and he left a gaping hole in their lives.

Later that year, I was visiting my niece the summer and she told me about a dream she recently had.

In the dream, her dad, my brother, came to her and showed her that he was with her at all the important milestones in her life; prom, high school graduation, her marriage, and the birth of her children. She felt him so intensely in the dream and she, too, woke up crying out of pure joy.

His spirit had been released and he could now comfort his daughters in a way he could not do until that moment.

The healing that has happened in my family because of this

work I have chosen to do is beyond anything I could have imagined. Whatever impulse or inner inspiration had led me on this path, I am forever grateful.

Helping our loved ones with this knowledge creates a deeper understanding of why we chose to be family.

Chapter Three

SPIRITS PASSED ON FROM PREVIOUS GENERATIONS

Spirits can stay with us from lifetime to lifetime, but they can also be passed from generation to generation.

One of my first experiences of this was with my husband. To tell this story, I need to share a little background.

Shortly after starting to meditate on a regular basis, I began having clairvoyant dreams. Clairvoyance is the ability to see beyond the physical realm. The dreams I have usually give me information for someone else that is important for them to know about.

One night, I had one of my most vivid, lucid dreams. In the dream, I walked into a small home. I looked around at the walls of the home and they were stacked from floor to ceiling with garbage. I noticed a hallway and walked towards it. When entering the hallway, I saw that it led to another, smaller room. I could not walk into the room, however, because the garbage on the walls made it too narrow for me to walk through.

I could see two figures in the room; a man and a woman. I could not see any other door or windows in the room and the question that came to mind was, "How did they get there and how will they get out?"

The dream was so vivid and real that I can still see the house, the garbage piled along the walls, the hallway and the two people stuck inside.

A few days later, my husband, Tony, had a personal session with Marie Diamond on one of her trips to our city. During the session, Tony found out that the two spirits I saw in my dream were attached to his energy field.

It turned out they had been handed down through his family generations for over five hundred years and they had been waiting for someone to see them and release them.

During the session, the two souls communicated what happened and how they came to be attached to my husband:

About five hundred years ago, a husband and wife were living a life as shamans in Siberia and had two children. Their village was attacked and they were brutally murdered in front of their children.

One of the children, a daughter, went into a state of shock. The overwhelming emotion of grief and despair at witnessing her parents' murders created an emotional attachment, which didn't allow their souls to move on from the experience.

What happened after that lifetime was remarkable. The child grew up, married and had children but was never able to release the emotional trauma from the experience of watching her parents being brutally murdered.

When she passed, the spirits of her parents were passed onto one of her children who continued to feel the emotional heaviness and grief that kept them stuck. These souls continued to be passed from generation to generation until they were finally passed to my husband.

The "garbage" I saw in my dream that covered the walls was all of the collected emotional energy that continued to keep them stuck. Carrying these souls for five hundred years made the person depressed, and as the emotional energy continued to build generation after generation, the depression worsened.

The carrier of these souls before they were passed to my husband was his father. His father had suffered from depression most of his life and after his dad passed, my husband began suffering from depression as well.

Once the souls were released, Tony remembered a dream he had several weeks after his father died in 1980. In the dream, Tony's father came to him and said, "I'm sorry son, I couldn't do it. You'll have to finish it."

Tony had no idea what this message meant back in 1980 but from the perspective of this new information received twenty-three years later, it made total sense.

Each person in each generation had hoped to find someone who was able to "see" these souls and help them to be released. The road to freedom for these two souls began when my husband and I met. We cannot always see the reasons two people meet and it is important to remember that there is more to a relationship than meets the eye.

We have the ability to reach beyond space and time and heal deep family wounds.

FINDING LOST SOUL PIECES

After I began working in groups to help spirits to be released, I began to attract clients who had a soul piece that needed to be released from past traumatic experiences.

> *Soul piece: A part of our soul that incarnates into a body during a specific lifetime. Our soul is multidimensional and exists in various realms of existence simultaneously.*

Before I share a few of their stories, I think it is important to understand more about soul aspects, why they get stuck and the importance of the soul retrieval work that so many people are engaged in at this time.

When a Soul Gets Stuck

To understand soul retrieval, it is important to know that each of us has a soul or spirit aspect that is outside of the physical experience. Each of us started in a field of oneness. Over time, the separation of the soul from this field of oneness has occurred.

A simple explanation of this is to think of who you are in total connection to the Universe or to the field of oneness. You can also think of it as the parent.

The soul, or parent, sends out an aspect of itself to incarnate or come into a body. Each time an aspect of the soul incarnates, it gains more understanding of who they are as a soul.

Many believe we incarnate to learn certain lessons during a lifetime and earth is the school where we come to learn these lessons. These lessons include learning how to trust, forgive, surrender, and express love.

When our life is over, we have a chance to review our time here and see what we did that expanded our light and the light of others. We also get to see what we did that depleted our light and the light of others. These are referred to as dharmic and karmic lifetimes. Did we create more density for ourselves and others, or did we create more light?

But sometimes, at the end of a lifetime, the soul does not return to the oversoul, or parent soul. Our light was sent out (incarnated in a body) and when the body died, the spirit did not return. Instead, it got stuck because of some experience that happened during that particular lifetime.

> *Oversoul: a term used to describe both the expansiveness of our own soul/spirit and our connection to the field of oneness.*

When that lifetime ended, the emotional trauma, shock or some type of attachment kept us from seeing the doorway to leave. We stayed in this plane of existence instead of leaving and returning to the parent soul to continue our soul evolution.

Soul retrieval is the process of retrieving that soul piece from the experience that kept it stuck and then creating a doorway for it to leave, if it chooses to.

This is such important work for us to be doing, because as long as a soul piece is stuck in this dimension, it cannot continue in its evolution. There is a piece of us that stops our own spiritual evolution and we cannot completely return to the field of oneness until every aspect of our soul is brought home.

Each time I release spirits, either individually or in a group clearing, I know that someone is getting an aspect of their soul returned to them. We can't always see or know the full impact this has on humanity, but I trust that humanity is evolving because of it.

Chapter Five
SHARON'S STORY

I received a phone call one day from a woman named Sharon. She had heard about the work I do and asked me to dowse her home she had just moved into. She knew there was something going on as both her and her son started having health issues shortly after moving in.

After dowsing and space clearing the home, I was guided to connect with Sharon to do a space clearing of the land as well. The space clearing session was done over the phone as I was in living in North Dakota at the time and Sharon's home was in Arizona.

As we began the session, Sharon shared with me that as they were moving into the home, she glimpsed a Native American chief out of the corner of her eye. She had not seen him before that time and felt he was there to tell her something.

Immediately after bringing her into connection with the land and bringing light into the property, Sharon began to feel sick. I connected with the chief, knowing he was there to help us.

What we began to witness was very similar to my first group space clearing meditation; souls stuck because of an event that had happened. As we brought in more light, the events began to unfold. We saw the chief gather the souls of his people and hold them in that place until someone would come along to help release them.

Sharon then began to see herself in the event as a young woman. She was hiding behind a large boulder and next to her was her younger brother who she recognized as her son in this lifetime.

From their hiding space, they witnessed the massacre of their tribe and she began to tremble in fear. They hid in that place, with Sharon protecting her young brother, until the attackers left and they could run to safety.

As we continued with the healing, Sharon saw her and her brother's souls reconnect with their Native American father, who was the chief. We both helped the chief release the heavy emotional energy and shock that had kept them stuck. Once the emotional energy was released, we held the space as the chief ushered the souls through the portal that had been opened for them.

It became very clear to both Sharon and I that she had been attracted to that area and to the house because her and her son's soul had some healing to do. But they were also instrumental in helping the souls who were stuck in that experience.

Once the healing happened and the souls were released, both Sharon and her son quickly returned to health.

The healing of our bodies can be intimately connected with the healing of the land.

Chapter Six

NATIVE AMERICAN SPIRITS

Another experience of releasing Native American spirits blew me away. It turned out that I had a soul piece that was involved in the event that I had been called to help.

A couple living outside of the Fargo area asked me to dowse their home. They had moved into the home about eight years earlier and started getting sick after moving in. By the time I came to dowse, both had severe illnesses and doctors could not find a cause. This was especially troubling for the couple as they led a very healthy lifestyle in so many ways.

When I walked into their home, which was ten miles out of town, I was surprised to find it filled with Native American artifacts, pictures and original pieces. It was beautiful and I felt I had stepped back in time.

A short time before this appointment, I had learned about karma lines and how clearing them helps release the karma that attracted a person, couple or an entire family to a home. I found two karma lines for the couple, one for each of them.

As soon as I placed the cures, a huge wave of emotional energy released from the house and the land. I was overtaken with these emotions and had no idea what had caused the energy that was being released.

I asked the owners for a quiet room where I could begin to tune into the energy being released and to see what had created it.

After releasing the emotional energy, I saw a massacre of a tribe of Native Americans. I also saw the couple currently living in the house as the chief and his wife who had lived on this land before.

Sadly, they had taken on the guilt and responsibility for allowing this happen to their people. They were devastated.

During this very special clearing, I was given new information that I continue to use each time I help Native spirits release. The first step I received was to create a ceremony to help them leave.

This included calling in a large white teepee, which would become an energetic doorway, a portal, to leave.

Portal: An energy field created with the use of light frequencies with the intention of connecting the third dimensional field to the fourth and fifth dimensional fields, making it easy for souls to transition from one dimension to another.

Shortly after I called in the white teepee, Native drummers and dancers appeared to help hold the space and prepare the spirits for their transition into another dimension.

The ceremony that ensued was beautiful to watch. As I continued to help them release their karma, the dense energy began to dissipate. Souls began to find each other and join hands. When everyone was awake and connected, they entered the teepee to continue their soul journey.

The last ones to leave were the spirits of the chief and his wife. They stood at the door of the teepee until the last soul had left. They then stepped into the teepee themselves. The home and land became very peaceful and filled with light. I knew it was healed.

I left the room that I was space clearing and walked into the main area of the house. Simultaneously, the husband was coming out of one of the rooms. When I saw him, I recognized him as the chief and immediately knew we were friends from this previous lifetime. Tears of joy and recognition filled my eyes.

I saw that I was a white man in that lifetime and we had befriended each other. The last time I had seen him was on a visit where I tried to warn him about the danger that was heading his way. He didn't listen to my warning. It resulted in the massacre of his people.

I now realized why there were so many emotions for me around the clearing of these souls. In truth, they had been my friends in a previous lifetime.

The last thing that happened made this particular experience one of the most memorable of all that I have done so far.

After updating the couple about what I found and cleared from their land, they finally understood why they were drawn to that house and why they became sick after moving there.

They then showed me a picture that was hanging above their bed. It was an old photograph of a Native American chief and his wife and I recognized the people in the picture as the people standing in front of me. They had actually found a photograph of themselves and slept under that picture each night!

A Happy Ending

When doing this work, I always trust that something will be transformed in the lives of the people I connect with. The transformation was powerful for this couple. They released the energy from their past experience and let go of all the guilt they were holding onto.

I happened to see them about five years later and hardly recognized them. They were both in vibrant health and during our brief visit, they informed me that they had just purchased motorcycles and were starting a cross-country trip.

I knew at that moment they had completely released and healed from the karmic lifetime that had drawn them to that property and triggered their illnesses.

Healing happens in many ways and being open to new possibilities will quicken the healing.

Chapter Seven

PAST LIFE ENERGY IN PRESENT TIME

I was teaching a class in Ashland, Oregon and received a call from a single woman in her 60's. She couldn't attend the class but asked me to come over to clear the negative energy in her home.

Just like the couple in the previous chapter, she had moved into the home twelve years prior and very quickly became ill. The home was in one of the more established areas of the city and was built in the early 1900's.

Prior to meeting her, she had been spending a lot of time, energy and money trying to find a solution to her health problems but nothing had changed. In fact, she had become even sicker.

When scheduling the appointment, I asked her what was happening in her space. She informed me that after moving in, she had set up her art studio in the detached, converted garage. However, once it was set up, every time she spent any time in the space, she would become very emotional, depressed and feel sick. The house felt a bit better after dowsing, but she decided to stop trying to spend time in the studio and had to give up her love of creating artwork.

When I arrived a week later for the appointment, she met me at the door and was somewhat shaken. The reason for her shakiness was a dream she had the night before I arrived.

She said her dream felt very real and was able to describe it in great detail. She saw herself as a young girl living with her parents in the house she now lived in. Here is what she shared with me:

"I was a girl of eleven years old and was in the garage one afternoon (the now converted garage). As I was playing there, my sixteen-year old cousin came in and I was happy to see him. But he had a different reason for coming into the garage and I ended up being raped.

I was traumatized and that night, my parents knew something was wrong with me. When pressed, I told them what had happened.

My parents and extended family met and chose to not punish my cousin but to, instead, accuse a young black man who lived close to us. The family went to his house, accused him of the crime and without any trial, brought him to a place outside of town and hung him. I remember standing with my parents as they made me watch this horrible scene."

As she spoke, she was visibly shaking and started crying uncontrollably. She knew without a doubt that she had lived in this home before this lifetime and what she saw in her dream had happened in the converted garage. She also understood why she could not spend time in that space.

In this situation, I knew that along with the dowsing of her home, I also needed to do some clearing work for her as well.

As I energetically connected with her, I felt a very heavy energy attached to her. It turned out that the soul of the young black man had attached to her after he died and she still carried him with her. During the session, she was helped in releasing both her own guilt and pain from the experience, as well as the soul that she had been carrying since her previous lifetime.

The negative energy from the trauma of the rape was also

released. Her healing had begun. Over time, she was able to return to creating her artwork in a space free of the trauma of her past life experience.

We have the opportunity in this lifetime to heal the traumas created in past life experiences.

Chapter Eight

SPIRITS USED AS ENTERTAINMENT

Two separate events happened before I learned how to release spirits. Looking back, it is apparent that I had done this work in previous lifetimes, as my soul stepped into the work without a conscious intention from my personality.

In both experiences, I encountered people who were using the spirits as some form of entertainment. Even before I started connecting with this work, something didn't feel right about spirits being used in this way.

The first event happened at a weekend retreat I was attending. The retreat focused on helping the attendees become aware of their psychic abilities. The weekend was great until Saturday evening when the retreat facilitator took the group to her cabin outside of the city. We were told it was full of spirits and we would have a magical encounter with them.

After eating our evening meal, she asked us to sit around a large table. She began a ceremony where she invited the spirits to join us. She then asked the group to open and receive one of the spirits to communicate through us.

The retreat leader seemed very proud to be in possession of these spirits and we were told that all the participants of every retreat were brought to this experience.

I don't remember the messages that came through at this point and I'm sure some may have been insightful, but I couldn't get over the feeling that these spirits were trapped in that place, doing what they were asked to do until someone came along to help them.

The night ended and we all went to bed.

During the night, I was aware of a lot of activity happening but wasn't sure what was going on. The group gathered to resume the retreat at nine a.m. the next morning but the retreat leader was not there. When she finally appeared sometime after ten a.m., she was very tired and a bit confused. She said she had a very restless night and I knew immediately that her soul had participated in the release of the spirits.

As the group tuned into the energy of the house that morning, we all knew the spirits had left. I felt an inner joy knowing that they would no longer be used as part of a paid retreat experience.

The next time it happened, I was much more aware of my role in assisting in the release of souls. This came as a result of stepping into my soul's purpose.

I was traveling and was invited to stay with some friends. They were both artists and very proud to show me their home and artwork. On the tour of their home, they brought me into a room where they said they did a lot of entertaining. They then went on to inform me that the house was haunted and they had several spirits living with them who usually hung out in this room.

Once or twice a month, they would invite their friends over to hang out with these spirits and to see who could see them or have some kind of experience. Their friends loved it and they were known for the "spirit encounter" evenings.

That night after going to sleep, I had a night full of lucid dreaming as I was connecting with the souls of the owners of the house. I saw myself communicating with them about the importance of releasing these spirits and helping them let go of any attachments they had to them which kept them in their house.

At one point in the dream, I opened a portal for the spirits to be released and I watched them leave. The next morning when I woke, the spirits were gone.

There was no discussion about the events that happened during the night. I'm not sure they were conscious or aware of the work that took place while they slept but I knew on a soul level, they had agreed to help the spirits release from this dimension.

I wasn't around to see how their personalities reacted when they could no longer use the spirits for their "spirit encounter" evenings but it didn't matter. The spirits were back where they belonged.

Helping our spirit brothers and sisters go home is the best choice when given the opportunity

Chapter Nine

TRAVELING SPIRITS

One day I received a phone call from a friend in Oregon asking for help. Her three-year-old granddaughter was seeing spirits in the closet of her room and they needed help releasing them.

My friend was open to learning about spirit release so I energetically connected with her and brought her into the meditation to help release them.

The spirits were a man and woman who were there, not to be released but to bring us a message. As I connected with them and listened to their story, they gave us information about a tragic fire that happened years ago and they were there to help their friends. In this situation, I felt we needed to confirm their story to know the location of the trapped spirits.

My friend, who has lived in Oregon most of her life, began searching for tragic fires that happened in a 100-mile radius of her granddaughter's house. She found and shared a news article of a fire that happened on Christmas Eve in 1907 in Silver Lake, Oregon. You can read the news article about this event in the Resources page in the back of this book.

The people of a small town had gathered in a room above the school for their traditional Christmas Eve program. During the program, an oil lamp was bumped, spilling the oil and instantly ignited the room on fire. There was only one exit from the room and with the panic that ensued, 43 people lost their lives. Every family in the small town was affected.

As we read the news article, chills ran through us. We knew these were the souls that were asking for our help.

Another friend asked to be a part of the clearing work and we scheduled a time to meet over the phone. We connected first with the spirits that found us and followed them to where the souls were trapped in and around the school.

The energy we felt was heavy with grief. It felt like a dark, wet blanket over the souls. We immediately began to clear this energy and the area in and around the school started to feel lighter.

Along with the two souls that found us, another soul started to help awaken the trapped souls. It was one of the teachers of the school and we watched as she began helping the others. One by one the souls found each other. As the energy continued to transform, the area shifted from a heavy blanket of grief to celebration. They were ready to go home.

We opened a portal for them to leave and witnessed the teacher leading everyone into it. She was the last to leave.

The celebration continued as the souls were welcomed by their families and friends waiting for them on the other side.

We continued to be in awe of the two souls who ventured so far in hopes of finding someone who could help their families and friends.

An Afterthought

It occurred to me after this particular clearing session that the publishing of the article itself helped open the energy so that these souls could go home. It was just four short years after the article was published that the souls were released. Our conscious awareness of an event is sometimes enough to begin the process of healing.

When we open our hearts and listen, we are led to where we are needed

Chapter Ten

WHAT KEEPS SPIRITS STUCK?

The reasons the souls of people do not move on after death are as varied as the souls themselves.

When I help individual souls release, there is usually some emotion, trauma, shock, fear or deep grief that keeps them from moving on at the time of their death. In some cases where drugs or alcohol was a large part of a person's life, such as the case of the previous owner of my house, there was so much energetic fog around them that they were not able to see where to go when leaving their physical bodies.

At times, an energetic cord is created that keeps the person or group of people from leaving.

This energetic cord can be created by the person who died or by the people they left behind. It is usually emotional in nature and prevents the spirit from moving on.

If the dying person feels like they cannot leave their loved ones or if they feel any kind of guilt or remorse, it can create an attachment. The soul can also choose to stay behind, as in the case of my brother, until its karma is cleared with someone. When the karmic connection is released, they will no longer attract that soul or karmic experience into their future incarnations.

Many cultures believe that a soul has many lifetimes and that it moves on to continue learning, evolving and experiencing their soul in another dimension. When a society believes that the soul only has one lifetime, however, it makes it more difficult for the people to let go of the soul or for the soul to move on.

Any emotion of anger, fear, grief, guilt or hatred can create an attachment that connects a soul with a person or place. The story in Chapter Seven is a good example of this. An eleven-year-old child watched the hanging of a man wrongly accused of raping her and she was helpless to do anything about it. The anguish she felt towards this man was so strong, her emotions created an energetic bond, or attachment, and as he left his body, she wasn't able to let him go. They were then locked together in a karmic connection where both needed to forgive the actions of the people around them.

Forgiveness is always the key in releasing spirits from this world. But sometimes, before forgiveness happens, they need to share their story and their pain with those holding the space for them. The space, when held with non-judgment and unconditional love, is crucial when helping our brothers and sisters move on from this world.

Group Spirits that are Stuck

When a group of souls are asking for help, I don't see attachments as much as the energy the group created at the time of their death.

When an entire group creates the energy of fear, shock, anger or grief, it is much stronger because the entire group experienced it.

It doesn't take much to imagine the trauma, fear or emotional shock felt by an individual or group of people going through a horrific experience. We read about terrifying events of people being killed by a gunman or explosions in nightclubs. These types of events have happened throughout the history of humanity.

All of the emotions experienced during these occurrences create a dense energy field for this group of souls. They cannot see their way out of the density in order to leave this dimension. The soul leaves the body thinking this is all there is, and they forget they are a soul that can continue their journey once they leave this dimension. The emotional trauma is bigger than anything else at that moment.

When I tap into this energy, it looks very much like a heavy coat covering the souls. This heavy coat of energy is what keeps the spirits asleep or stuck in the experience. I use light frequencies to help spirits release from this energy. Light frequencies help to remove the layers of emotional energy or attachments so the souls can begin to 'wake up.'

When working with groups of souls, there are usually one or two souls that awaken first. It's like watching a flower unfold as each soul represents a petal of the flower. I see them find each other, help each other wake up and prepare to leave.

At some point in the process, they see the portal that has been created for them and when everyone is ready, they step into the doorway. And very similar to a high-speed elevator, they are transported back to wherever in the universe their soul needs to be, to continue its evolution.

Our souls will transition with ease when we release our own attachments to places, people and things during our lifetime

Chapter Eleven
HELPING SPIRITS GO HOME

The spirits I have worked with over the years have needed help in letting go of something that was keeping them from seeing the portal. Once the energy was cleared, they were able to see it and leave.

There are also spirits ready to leave, in fact, *waiting* to leave and simply need someone who knows how to help them.

In one of my first space clearing sessions, the group sat in a circle and was guided into a meditation to become energetically protected as a portal was created in the center of the group. As soon as the portal was created, the spirits began to enter the circle. The group continued to hold the space and over two hundred spirits stepped into the portal. Adult, child and even animal spirits entered. It looked and felt to everyone in the group that the spirits were stepping into a "quantum elevator" that took them to their next soul experience.

It took a mere twenty minutes before all of the spirits were gone. Afterwards, the room, the building and the entire area felt lighter and clearer.

So where did these spirits come from and how did they know to show up at that place and time

There is something called "spirit communication" where messages are sent out, consciously or unconsciously, and are received by the spirits.

Opening a portal to release a group of spirits can be compared to a train pulling into the station and everyone on the platform gets in. They have resolved whatever kept them from leaving when they died and they are now ready to leave this dimension. If they are not ready, they will wait for a future opportunity. It is up to us to create enough opportunities for the spirits that are ready and waiting to leave.

My passion is releasing groups of spirits, especially when I am helping spirits that are in need of help.

This can be done to help individual souls or groups of souls. Both involve quieting, listening, tuning into what is needed by the soul(s) and holding space for them as they release whatever energy is keeping them stuck. Once this happens, they can then see the portal and the souls that are waiting for them in the next dimension.

The group work I do usually takes place during a class. When a group gathers to do this work, someone in the group receives information about where a group of souls need our help. This information may come in a dream, a conversation with someone or something heard or seen on TV, radio or in a book.

As a group, we then focus on helping the souls release the pain, trauma, shock or emotional energies keeping them stuck.

During this process, an interesting phenomenon will sometimes happen.

As the energy is released, one or more of the people in the group "see" themselves in the event that is being released. They begin reliving the experience and can feel the emotional energy being released from their own bodies. The rest of the group continues to support those moving through this releasing process.

One group experience led us to a group of souls that were part of a native tribe who were massacred by a surprise attack.

One woman in our group saw herself as a pregnant mother, holding a young child. The emotions of grief and anger at what was happening to them was overwhelming, along with a sense of powerlessness of not being able to protect her child. All of these emotions had remained locked inside of her until we began the clearing work.

Once the energy that had kept them stuck was released, the souls stepped into the portal. The people who had seen themselves as part of the experience returned to a peaceful state. Most also had a sensation or knowing that an aspect of their soul had been returned to them. They felt more expanded, lighter and somehow changed.

After this phenomenon continued to happen, I couldn't help but wonder how many people who were not present in the group felt when their soul pieces were released and returned to them.

These kinds of experiences have given our groups a very real experience of how such strong emotional energy can keep a group of souls trapped in their experience and unable to leave.

It also gave me a deeper understanding and appreciation of the work we are being called to do for humanity.

How many spirits are waiting for us to wake up to their presence?

Chapter Twelve

HITCHHIKER SPIRITS

Spirits don't always wait for someone to release them. Instead, they may travel to find a soul who is willing to help. I call these hitchhiker spirits as they will attach to someone and hitch a ride to where they want to go.

I have a grandson who will occasionally bring home a spirit that needs some help. His mother has learned how to recognize when this happens because her son's personality changes. Her easygoing, happy son becomes sad, angry or defiant as the emotional energy of the spirit who attaches to him takes over.

As I help the spirit release this energy, the story of why they got stuck comes to light.

One especially poignant experience happened when I was helping the spirit of a six-year-old boy who attached to my grandson. As I was helping him leave, I felt he was carrying a lot of anger in his energy field. The story unfolded to reveal what had happened right before he died. He had become angry with his dad and left the house on his bike. As he headed to a nearby park, he was hit by a car and died.

The anger he held towards his dad kept him from seeing the

portal to leave. I helped him release the anger and also forgive his dad for being angry with him. Once this energy was cleared, he saw the portal, stepped into it and was greeted by the spirit of a grandparent.

The anger that was keeping the spirit from leaving had taken over my grandson's emotions. Once the emotional energy and the spirit were released, he was able to be his own happy self again.

Not all hitchhiker spirits will affect the energy of the person carrying them. Some have resolved what kept them stuck and are just ready to leave. The challenge is simply to find someone who can help them.

My daughter and I had spent a week visiting my mom at the rehabilitation center and then drove back to Minneapolis. After my daughter left to go home, I started seeing a spirit out of the corner of my eye.

With all of my experience of releasing spirits, I questioned how a spirit could have entered my space. It took a few days to realize that a spirit from the rehab center had attached to my daughter. She must have dropped him off at my house so I could release him.

Upon realizing this was happening, I opened a portal and he immediately left. He didn't need any help releasing the energy that had kept him stuck in the first place as he had released it already. He simply needed to find someone who knew how to open a portal.

This kind of experience happens to some people after learning how to release spirits. Their hearts are open and willing to assist. However, they are slightly unnerved by the experience the first couple of times until they realize that the spirits are finding them because they know how to help them.

The feeling of knowing they are helping these spirits is immensely rewarding.

When you step into your soul purpose, spirits that need your help will find you.

Chapter Thirteen

RELEASING ANIMAL SPIRITS

Humans are not the only ones who get trapped in this dimension. Animals can also have a traumatic experience and get stuck.

Much of the time when a portal is opened for the souls of humans, animal spirits show up as well. Once in awhile, I am called to release a large group of animals that need help. This happened for a group of buffalo souls.

The situation came to light when I was meeting with a group of moms whose children had all attended a school together in the northeast part of my city.

After meeting them and getting to know them, a few started sharing how the energy of the school was a bit heavy. Something was creating some tension and chaos between the teachers of the school.

When I checked into the energy of the school and the grounds, I could see a lot of darkness and felt a wave of overwhelming emotions. It turned out to be a herd of buffalo that needed some help passing over. I shared this information with the group and we then scheduled a time to meet and help these souls be released.

One of the moms went home and shared this information with her nineteen-year-old daughter who immediately told her mom of a recurring dream she had since she was seven-years old.

In the dream, she was with a herd of buffalo. One of the buffalo would come to her and kneel down so she could ride on its back. When she climbed on, her and the buffalo would lead the herd through the plains, running at high speed.

After a short time, however, the herd began to slow down and came to a very heavy, gray place. When they reached the edge of this place, the herd became lifeless as they continued to walk through. And this is where her dream always ended.

She continued to have this dream about once a year and although she felt a strong connection and compassion for the buffalo, she didn't know how to help them. When her mom told her that we were meeting to do just that, she was excited and came to add her light and energy to the group.

Eight of us gathered one warm, Monday morning at one of the homes close to the school. Now that we knew the buffalo needed some help, everyone was ready and willing to be a part of this. No one in the group had done this kind of work before but they were all open to be guided into the meditation and to hold the space for healing to happen.

A very important first step when doing any kind of spirit release work is to prepare our own energy field. This means to get out of the ego, connect with higher states of awareness and most importantly, create an energetic shield of protection. When I guide a group in this work, there are steps we move through to protect and prepare ourselves for this sacred work.

The group felt calm and connected to the field of oneness by the time we were ready to connect with the buffalo spirits. The meditation was beautiful as the group held a space of unconditional love for them.

When they were ready, we opened a portal and after a few

gingerly checked it out, the rest charged into it, knowing they were going home.

During the meditation, I asked the people present to share what they were seeing, hearing or feeling as each person's soul connects with a different part of the process.

After a space-clearing meditation, I also provided time and space for sharing. At that time, the young woman with the recurring buffalo dreams shared the experience she had during the meditation. Here is what she shared with the group:

Shortly after connecting with the buffalo herd, a large white buffalo came in front of her and thanked her for being there. The recurring dream then started playing out again. One of the buffalo knelt down so she could climb on his back and they led the herd just like in her dream.

This time was a bit different, however, because a portal appeared. Instead of the herd running forward, they began circling the portal. They ran around it several times until the buffalo she was riding headed into it. The next few followed tentatively, found it to be safe and the rest entered with reckless abandon.

She continued to be on the back of the head buffalo and what she saw brought tears to her eyes. As she entered the portal on the back of a buffalo, she saw a beautiful, green pasture surrounded by rolling hills and streams. It was heaven for the herd of buffalo.

She was again thanked by the head buffalo and was told she could not stay with them; it was time for her to leave. She exited the portal and saw herself again with our group.

Everyone in the group was in tears as she shared her experience with us. We knew without a doubt that the buffalo spirits were home and would never have to walk through the dark valley again.

Human spirits are not the only ones needing our help

Chapter Fourteen

COMMUNICATING WITH SPIRITS

On the first day of teaching one of my dowsing classes, just a few hours after we began, I realized that something was off. The students weren't able to get their dowsing rods to work and there seemed to be a lot of interference and confusion around us.

When I tuned into the space, I "saw" the meeting room and hallways filled with spirits. I knew immediately that they were showing up, knowing they were going to be released. But this was scheduled to happen at the end of the weekend and not during the first morning of the class.

I quickly understood that I did not communicate the schedule of events to the spirits. I didn't let them know to stay out of the space until 4 p.m. on Sunday when a portal would be opened for them.

It was too late to move them outside of the building so the weekend schedule was changed and I taught the space clearing part of the weekend first. Once the spirits were released, everyone was able to use their dowsing rods and the rest of the weekend went as planned.

It was an important first lesson for me, and one I continue to teach as I help others communicate with the spirit world.

We need to learn the importance of communicating with beings in other dimensions

Chapter Fifteen

PEOPLE WHO ATTRACT SPIRITS

One day I received a phone call from a woman who had heard about me and was interested in my work with spirits.

She called me because spirits were continually finding her, day and night, and asking to be released. She wasn't sleeping very well as they would disturb her in the middle of the night and she felt she could not even work or move on with her life because of them. Her entire existence was helping spirits cross over, and there was no one to pay her for what she was doing.

During our initial conversation, I saw her as someone who had done this work in past lifetimes. When she came into this lifetime, she did not take a class or need be trained on how to release spirits. She just knew how to do it because she had done it before.

What she needed help with was to learn how to set some boundaries with the spirits that were coming to her. She wanted to learn a new, upgraded program to send them home. In the past, people who were here to help wandering spirits used their own energy fields to help them. These people were connected with their own light and the light of the universe, which provided a doorway to release these spirits. Spirits can see when people have this ability and are drawn to them, looking for help.

This way of releasing spirits becomes very draining, however, and just like this woman, people spend their time doing nothing else.

When we use our own energy fields to release spirits, we might take on some energy of the spirit we are helping to release. This can create many long-term health problems, especially if we don't know how to keep our own energy fields cleared.

There were three things this woman needed if she was going to continue releasing spirits.

One was to protect her energy field and create personal boundaries for herself and her home. Second, to learn how to communicate with spirits and to trust that they would listen to her when she sent them a message. And the third was to open up a doorway for these spirits to be released and direct them to the portal, instead of her energy field.

What her life looked like after we worked together was totally different from her previous life.

First, she started to energetically protect her energy field and her home's energy field. This created an energetically boundary, or firewall, that communicated a message to the spirits that this was her space.

Then she started communicating with the spirits. She told them that she would be opening the portal each morning and to please line up at the perimeter of her property.

From that point on, each morning at 8 a.m. she would energetically protect herself and her home, open up a door in a quiet corner of her yard and invite the spirits to enter. She kept the portal open for fifteen minutes or until all of the spirits were gone.

Instead of releasing spirits as they came to her, she assured them they would be released at 8 a.m. the next morning and to please wait.

She was so happy that she could continue to help these spirits and still have a life of her own. By simply implementing a few new tools and enhancing awareness of spirit communication, her life was completely changed.

More efficient ways to be of service are always available

Chapter Sixteen

ANCESTOR SPIRITS

Somewhere along the way, my mother attained a certain level of comfort in the presence of spirits and did not go into fear when seeing one. In fact, she was very matter of fact about them.

This was helpful when spirits started showing up in her living room a few years ago.

What triggered their presence was her research into her family's genealogy. She had already been doing some research for about two years but as she dug deeper into her family's past, the spirits started showing up.

One day, as my mother was standing in her kitchen, looking out into the living room, she saw a woman standing in the center of her living room. The woman didn't say anything and just stood there, looking at my mom. My mom intuitively knew she was the great, great, great grandmother that she had recently found in her family's records.

The next spirit was a man and then another woman. They always appeared at the same place in her living room and always when she was in the kitchen looking out into the living room. And it always occurred after spending an extra amount of time on her family's genealogy.

No one else could see these spirits so she was hesitant to tell me about them. But when she finally did, I was able to help her understand why they were showing up and how she could help them.

These were spirits who had gotten stuck in this dimension and had been waiting for someone to know about them or "see" them, and who also had the ability to help them leave.

At the time, my mother didn't know how to help them, but she had a daughter who did. Spirits can see this and will show themselves when they see a possibility of being released.

My mother, at the age of seventy-nine, was very open to helping them. When I gave her the tools, she was happy to be able to help each of them transition out of this dimension.

When we start connecting with names, places and dates of our ancestors, we begin to bring them to life, so to speak. And when someone is able to actually see them, they will show up, asking for help. We don't always need to know why they were not able to leave this dimension when they died. However, when they show up, it means they are asking for help and ready to leave. They are happy someone is able to see them and release them.

Being in service is not dependent on a person's age or background

CHILDREN AND SPIRITS

I have witnessed a shift over the last twenty years in our society's belief in spirits. Some of this can be credited to the paranormal movies, TV shows and radio programs that people are watching and tuning into. Although other cultures have embraced the spirit world and the belief of disembodied spirits for ages, western civilization has been closed off to their existence. Many times, I see that it is the children that are opening people to their existence.

Many people I talk to report seeing spirits when they were children. But when they told their parents or someone else about what they were experiencing, they were told it was their imagination or that they were crazy. Many of these people eventually shut down and forced themselves to stop seeing spirits, as no one was around to help them understand the experience they were having. Other times they stayed connected but felt like oddities or freaks among their family and friends.

I'm sure this is still happening in some homes but I am encouraged by what I have seen the past ten years. There is more openness to listening to the child and believing them when they share their spirit encounters. What has changed dramatically is that parents are not discounting their child's experience, but are beginning to search for answers.

Parents are beginning to seek out people who can help their child (and the spirits) if they cannot help them themselves.

Most of the space clearing work I do is because of a child seeing something in the house that they begin talking about. Some children go into fear; some will act out while others will simply start talking about the man in the corner of the bedroom.

I was called to one house where a nine-year old child was seeing spirits in two rooms of the house. The child was not home when I came to dowse and the mother did not tell me where her daughter was seeing the spirits.

I found two areas in the lower part of the house. One in the bathroom and one in the playroom needed to be cleared. Afterwards, the mom shared with me that these were the exact two rooms that her daughter was seeing the spirits and was afraid to go into. Once the spirits were released, the daughter never mentioned them again and she was not afraid in any rooms of the house.

It was refreshing to see that the mom did not doubt her daughter's experience for a minute. Instead, she started to search for someone who could help. Thankfully, children are no longer being told it is "just their imagination" or that they are crazy. This means more and more children will grow into adulthood, staying connected with their gift of seeing beyond this reality.

There is still fear around the existence of spirits and a lack of understanding as to why they are in the house, but there is at least a belief that these spirits exist. We have come a long way from fifty years ago!

It is time to open up and allow our children to move us beyond fear

PART

THE LAW OF ATTRACTION

The law of attraction is a law of the universe that demonstrates how we create the things, events and people that come into our lives.

As we explore the spirit realm and how the information presented in this book affects our lives, it is important to gain an understanding of the Law of Attraction.

The first thing to remember about this law is that it is always at work, whether we are aware of it or not. As we become more aware of it, we can begin to use it to change our lives more consciously.

What most people understand about the Law of Attraction is that they can change their lives by changing their thoughts, feelings and actions. This is a good start and does help, but it certainly does not reveal all aspects entirely. When people do not have the complete picture, it is easy to become frustrated.

In 2006 the movie, *The Secret*, hit the self-help world. Within six months of the release of the movie, I started receiving calls from people telling me that they had watched the movie, did everything the movie suggested, but came to the conclusion that the Law of Attraction was not working for them. The level of frustration they were dealing with was extremely evident. This was because the information presented in the movie covered only one third of how it really works.

Each aspect presented in the next three chapters represents one third of our Law of Attraction. In the Chinese tradition, these aspects are described as luck and as something that doesn't just happen to us. They believe that we create our own luck when we understand and work with the three aspects of this law, which include Heavenly, Human and Environmental. All equally impact our Law of Attraction.

The information in the following chapters is based on the concept of the three Levels of the Law of Attraction created by Marie Diamond, built on the teachings of Feng Shui Grand Master Yap.

Understanding how the three aspects work, have transformed my own life and those who have received this information.

The Law of Attraction is always at work in our lives whether we are aware of it or not

Chapter Nineteen

LAW OF ATTRACTION ASPECT OF HEAVENLY LUCK

Heavenly Luck describes your soul's Law of Attraction. It is that aspect of you that reincarnates from lifetime to lifetime, bringing with it both karma and dharma. It is what has attracted you to where you were born, the parents and family you were born into and many of the positive and negative experiences you have had in your lifetime.

When exploring this aspect of the Law of Attraction, we have the opportunity to understand more about dharma and karma.

Dharma is the accumulation of gifts and talents you have acquired prior to and during this lifetime. These gifts may include the gift of healing, your natural artistic ability, telepathic ability or possibly the gift of being a peacemaker in your family or work place.

It is the vibration of your soul that attracts good things to you. Some might call it destiny and some call it just plain good luck. So where does this good luck come from?

When you have lived a previous lifetime in alignment with your soul's purpose and served humanity with your spiritual gifts, you have gained what some spiritual teachers refer to as golden marks. These golden marks accumulate over lifetimes and you have carried them with you into this lifetime. They create a certain vibration in your energy field and it attracts other high vibrations to you. Like attracts like.

There are times when souls carrying a high vibration meet at some point during this lifetime. When this happens, there is an instant connection as their vibrations match. Some of these souls begin collaborating and create something together in service to humanity.

Karma is the energy also created from past experiences and can create a density or heaviness in our bodies and energy fields.

We all have lifetimes where we created karma. Some were simply lifetimes where we remained stuck in a certain experience because of fear, grief, or limitations placed on us.

It is the accumulation of karma that creates some of your subconscious emotional and mental patterns that show up unexpectedly. Have you ever wondered why you react a certain way to someone you just met? What creates your fear of airplanes or fear of small places? Many times, you can thank the karma you were born with for these responses.

Your Heavenly Luck attracts people and circumstances into your life that gives you the opportunity to clear your karma and transform these experiences. You have the opportunity in this lifetime to release yourself from anything that is keeping you in a cycle of pain, grief, anger and density of any kind.

When you understand this aspect of the Law of Attraction, you will be more able to take responsibility for your life and realize that you have attracted every person and every experience into your reality. Once you accept responsibility, you are then able to graciously receive the "good luck" that happens in your life and change the "bad luck" that has come your way.

There is a popular quote that says, "When you're given lemons, make lemonade." This can be applied here as you take something that appears to be bad luck, see the silver lining or lesson in it, and turn it into something wonderful and transforming. I personally know many people who have done this over the past years as they lost jobs and homes. They looked at the experience, stayed out of the drama and decided it was a good time to start over.

It may be difficult to understand why we attract certain situations that are painful. But it is exactly what needs to happen if we are to release our karma and evolve and grow spiritually. Actually, it is a large part of why we chose to be here.

The best way to begin accessing your dharma and transforming your karma is through meditation or a spiritual practice. There are many wonderful spiritual practices available. Some are referenced in the back of this book.

We can change our spiritual Law of Attraction when we clear our karma and align with our dharma.

Chapter Twenty
LAW OF ATTRACTION ASPECT OF HUMAN LUCK

Human Luck is the energy that most people understand as the Law of Attraction.

Everything you do to improve yourself will change your Law of Attraction on this level. When you educate yourself, you expand your opportunities for a better job. When you exercise, you feel more motivated and energized to reach your goals. When you eat healthy food, you have more energy and health to fulfill your dreams. When you think positive thoughts, you create new pathways in your brain and begin to see the world differently.

I love movies that depict the main character going through a tough time, then ultimately transforms his or her life by taking positive action, or begins to see possibilities that they did not see before. They inspire and remind us that we have the choice to tap into these potentials within ourselves as well.

We all have the possibility to transform ourselves in some way. Along with inspirational movies, there are numerous TV programs that show how much interest there is in creating change in our lives. Current popular programs demonstrate ways to makeover our homes, our wardrobes and our bodies.

Most people who want to change what they attract in their lives begin with this aspect, as it is one of the easiest to understand and work with. This is reflected by the three billion dollars spent by Americans alone on self-improvement each year.

Taking action is an important step to improve our life

LAW OF ATTRACTION ASPECT OF ENVIRONMENTAL LUCK

Environmental Luck refers to the energy of your home or land that impacts your Law of Attraction, either positively or negatively.

Techniques such as space clearing, dowsing, and land blessings along with feng shui are ways that people are transforming the energy of their home and work environment, and thus, themselves.

Many cultures understood and used this knowledge. They found or created places on earth that energetically supported individuals as well as groups of people, to use this aspect of the Law of Attraction in a positive way. These groups included the Druids and Templars of Europe, Chinese Feng Shui masters and the Egyptians, as well as indigenous tribes including Aboriginals, Mayans, and Native American cultures.

You may have experienced the uplifting energy of places created by these cultures if you've visited sites like Stonehenge, Avebury, Machu Picchu, the pyramids of Egypt and the cathedrals of Europe. People are attracted to these well-known locations because they feel uplifted and inspired as the soul, human and environmental aspects align.

This aspect also refers to the locations on this planet where your soul is attracted and or connected. Chapters Five and Six give perfect examples of the Environmental Law of Attraction at work in people's lives. The individuals involved in these stories moved to an area where their soul had some healing to do from a past lifetime. At the time they moved, they had no idea their soul had guided them to that home. Once they settled in, however, the energy of the land began to trigger some deep subconscious memories. They began searching for a solution, only to find the discomfort that had surfaced was created in a past life experience.

These experiences, although uncomfortable and challenging, ultimately affected their Law of Attraction in a positive way as the healing brought a greater alignment between their soul, human and environmental aspects.

Not all energy in our homes that affects us negatively is created by a past life experience. There may also be energy in our home created by stress lines of the earth or man-made stresses. Symptoms of living in these types of energies can show up in our physical bodies. They can include poor sleep, nightmares, a weakened immune system, headaches and lack of focus.

After learning how to dowse, a woman discovered that two geopathic stress lines were the cause of her migraine headaches that she had been dealing with for fifteen years. Her headache immediately disappeared after curing the lines.

Because the negative energy of her home was cleared, she was then free to fulfill her life dreams and soul purpose.

Once you begin working with Environmental Luck through actions like dowsing, space clearing or feng shui, you will attract more of what you want in your life with ease.

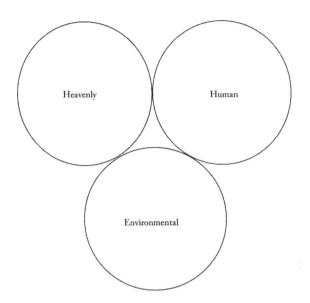

The Chinese refer to these levels as Heavenly Luck, Human Luck and Environmental Luck. They believe that we create our own luck.

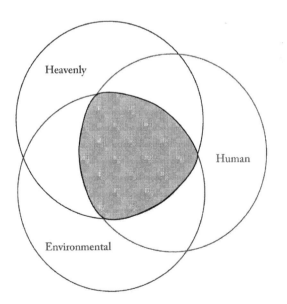

The more we work with all three levels, the more we become aligned. The more aligned we become, the more our life works for us.

Remembering our connection with the earth brings healing and wholeness

Chapter Twenty-Two

ANGELS, GUARDIAN SPIRITS AND SPIRITUAL MASTERS

When teaching people over the years about spirits that assist us, the terms angels, spirit guides and guardians are sometimes used interchangeably.

These beings can be largely misunderstood and there is good reason for it. When they appear in dreams or on the edge of our perception, we only use our limited human perspective to try to understand the encounter.

There are some distinct differences, however, as shown below.

Angels

When you think of angels, think of beings of light. These beings are usually known as messengers of the Divine realms and are here to serve. Although they may look male or female to us when they appear in a form, they are actually genderless and have never been in a human form.

Some are known as our guardian angels, with us from birth to death, and some appear at particular times in our lives to support, inspire and guide. They appear in some people's lives as a messenger bringing comfort, guidance or information.

Guardian Spirits

Guardian spirits, also known as spirit guides, are spirits who are assigned to us before we are born and help nudge and guide us through life. They are our spiritual team who we collaborated with before we incarnated. They have chosen to stay in the spirit realm to help us fulfill our spiritual contract, made before we were born.

A guardian spirit can also be someone who had a connection to us and who has an interest in our safety and wellbeing. They may be a deceased family member or ancestor who has taken an interest in us because of their relationship to us. It is not untypical for a grandparent to become a guardian spirit for a grandchild.

The difference between angels and guardian spirits is that guardian spirits were once incarnated in a physical body. They have either left their physical incarnation in this lifetime and continue to be with us, or have chosen not to incarnate in order to be in service in the spiritual realm.

Unlike angels, our guardian spirits can help us in ways that angels cannot. Having been human, they understand the unique challenges we face as humans who have chosen to incarnate on earth.

These guardian spirits can sometimes be animals. It is not unheard of for a spirit of a deceased animal to be seen watching over their beloved master.

Spiritual Masters

Spiritual Masters are what most people think of as Ascended Masters or Ascended Beings.

At the moment a soul awakens, a spiritual master connects with you to inspire and guide you in your spiritual evolution and work mainly in your dream states. However, they do appear to some people from time to time outside of dreams, such as in meditation or physical places on earth that are connected to the fifth dimension.

Until a soul releases at least 98% of their karma, they continue to reincarnate into a physical body. Once a soul has released most of their karma, they become freed from this karmic cycle and no longer need to reincarnate into a physical body.

The souls that have released this amount of their karma may continue their soul experience outside of a physical form and many will then become teachers for the souls still in human form. These are the souls many know as Ascended Masters.

Master Jesus, Buddha, Master Kuthumi, Lady Mary and Kuan Yin are just a few of the many known Ascended Masters.

These masters are spiritually enlightened beings who, in past incarnations, were ordinary humans but have experienced a series of spiritual transformations known as initiations.

The souls who have reached an initiation called Enlightenment are known as Enlightened Masters and those who have gone beyond their Enlightenment are known as Ascended Masters.

At this time in the evolution of humanity, we have both Enlightened and Ascended Masters who are incarnated and walking among us in human form. There are millions of Enlightened and Ascended beings on earth, teaching, healing, inspiring and helping to transform humanity and the planet. Because of the level they have reached in their evolution, they are aligned with their soul purpose and in service to the planet.

We Are Not Alone

It always brings me much comfort, knowing we are not alone. As the consciousness of humanity grows and expands, more people are beginning to see, feel and hear messages from beings that are guiding and supporting us along the way.

When we understand that we have a spiritual team with us during our lifetime, we can begin to consciously connect and be more open to their guidance and support.

We understand that we are always supported when we open ourselves to the guidance around us

Chapter Twenty-Three
WHAT DO SPIRITS LOOK LIKE?

Movies such as the *Sixth Sense*, that show mutilated and burned bodies are not an accurate depiction of what spirits look like after they pass. In my estimation, this has created a lot of fear because people feel they will be viewing gruesome images if they start seeing spirits.

In the years of doing this work, I have not seen any spirit look like what is shown in movies. If a spirit died of a stab wound and needs to be released, it does not appear to be with a knife in its chest. It simply presents as an energy form holding information of the event that occurred.

When I connect with them and begin releasing the trauma that has kept them stuck, the information about how they died begins to surface.

It is important that we do not confuse our physical bodies with our spirit bodies. When seeing through the eyes of our physical body, we experience things with the five physical senses of sight, sound, touch, smell and taste. When the spirit leaves the body, we need to engage our five spiritual senses to connect and communicate with the spirit world. Physical sight changes to spiritual sight and allows us to see beyond the physical body.

The memory of what happened to the physical body is stored in the spirit body but the physical act stays with the physical body.

There are certainly mediums who, when working with someone who is trying to connect with a loved one who has died, have had spirits reveal the way they died. When this happens, it is simply the spirit giving the medium information to confirm to the client that the spirit they are trying to contact is present.

For those with a desire to help, this is important to remember. Knowing that we will not be seeing a half burned body or mutilated corpse helps us more easily move from a place of fear to a place of love.

Remembering that the spirit body does not reflect the physical body sets us free from fear

Chapter Twenty-Four

THE IMPORTANCE OF HELPING EARTHBOUND SPIRITS

It is easy to think of spirits as beings outside of ourselves and not connected with us in any way. However, when we begin to understand that we exist in a field of oneness and we are all energetically connected, it changes our perspective.

We live in a time of fast evolutionary changes and the opportunity exists where our souls can evolve very quickly. As we evolve, we need to ask ourselves the question, "Do we really want to leave anyone behind?" It becomes personal to us when we consider that one of the trapped souls wandering the earth might be a parent, sibling or close friend that we knew in another lifetime.

Or, as in a few of the previous stories, one of the souls might even be an aspect of you! I have no doubt that an aspect of my own soul has been stuck in some kind of karmic event and someone has come along to give me a helping hand. I feel it is now my turn to do the same for others.

Another reason to help our spirit friends is because the energy that is keeping them stuck is holding the vibration of our planet and humanity at a lower level than what it could be.

If someone died while being tortured, the fear, hatred and painful emotions they experienced creates an energetic fog around them and their soul cannot see a way out of their experience. The strong emotions they created continue to keep them stuck until someone comes along to release them from this heavy energetic blanket. As we help them forgive the people who tortured them, they become able to reconnect to the light of their soul. Once they are freed from the experience that kept them trapped, they can continue their soul journey.

By transforming the heavy energy created by this experience and releasing the soul trapped in it, that part of the earth can become lighter and vibrate at a higher level.

This is especially powerful when a group of spirits is released. An entire area becomes filled with light and a higher vibration. (See Chapter 11 Helping Spirits Go Home).

When we help trapped spirits and clear the energy keeping them stuck, we uplift the energy of the planet

Chapter Twenty-Five

WHY DO THEY NEED OUR HELP TO LEAVE?

Some of the questions I often get asked are, "Why do souls need our help to be released? Why can't they just leave on their own?" or, "If there are angels, spirit guides and ascended masters around, why can't they help them?"

The answer is because angels, spirit guides and spiritual masters exist in the fifth dimension and if not embodied, cannot directly help an earthbound spirit. Their job is to inspire an awakened soul living in a physical body to gain the knowledge and the tools needed to help the earthbound spirits.

> *Earthbound: Attached or limited to material existence as distinct from a spiritual or heavenly one.*

Earthbound spirits cannot leave on their own because some energy or attachment is keeping them here. This creates an energetic fog, which can make it difficult see a way to the light. They need someone who is outside of the fog to help. Once this blanket of heavy energy is lifted or the attachment is released, they are able to connect once again with the light of their soul, remember who they are, and see the portal created for them to leave.

For this to happen, someone needs to be in a physical body to see them and help them. This person also needs to be conscious and connected to the light of his or her own soul. When someone is awakened to the light of their soul, they are living a fourth dimensional experience.

Third, Fourth, and Fifth Dimensions

The analogy I like to use to describe the third, fourth and fifth dimension is that of a seed in the ground. When the seed is just a seed, it exists under the surface of the earth and has no direct access to the sun. It exists in one dimension only and could be compared to the third dimension.

As the seed begins to grow and breaks through the topsoil, it then has access to the light of the sun and begins its journey into the fourth dimension. In this fourth dimensional experience, the seed becomes aware of who and what it is and the gifts contained inside of the seed start to become known. It continues to grow and expand until it reaches the fifth dimension where it blossoms and bears fruit. It is a fully realized seed and begins to share its gifts with the world.

A soul choosing to have a human experience comes here to remember itself as a soul. A soul who has not yet awakened, experiences life only in the third dimension. This means that the experiences they have are limited to the five physical senses of sight, touch, hearing, taste and smell. Anything that exists outside of the physical realm does not exist for them.

When a soul awakens, they have what is known as a heart opening experience; they reconnect and remember that they are a soul living in a human body. At this stage, they will now begin their journey experiencing the fourth dimension. Their five spiritual senses begin to awaken and they begin to see, feel, and hear what is beyond the physical realm.

When a soul continues to live more fully in the fourth dimension, with their hearts open and their spiritual senses awakened, they become conduits, or connectors, between the third and fifth dimensions.

Earthbound spirits need us, in fact are waiting for us, to acquire tools to help them. Not everyone is called to help, of course, but we do need more people willing to help our earthbound soul brothers and sisters.

We become the connectors between dimensions when we awaken to our soul purpose

COMMUNICATING WITH EARTHBOUND SPIRITS

The ability to communicate with an earthbound spirit is an ability that comes naturally for some and develops over time for others. As the spirit is no longer in a body and does not have a personality to communicate with, we need to develop our other senses in order to connect with them.

The easiest way to connect with an earthbound spirit is through the vibration of love. When we stay in a place of unconditional love, it sends a message of comfort and safety to those we are trying to connect with.

Love is the key that unlocks doors closed by fear, anger or grief. The soul that is trapped feels this vibration and responds.

To stay in a place of love, it is important to quiet the personality. This means that we need to learn how to calm the emotions and quiet the mental chatter. Feelings and thoughts of fear and doubt keep us disconnected from the vibration of love. Once the personality is quiet, we can more easily access our soul and hold a higher vibration for the soul or souls we are trying to help.

> *Personality: the combination of characteristics or qualities that form an individual's distinctive character. An aspect of ourselves, created by emotional and mental expressions and patterns.*

Communicating with earthbound spirits happens beyond the personality. The information we receive may not come in the normal way we are used to communicating. It may come in visuals, a feeling or simply a knowing. We all have our own experience when beginning to communicate on this level. The different ways to receive information are known as clairaudience (hearing), clairvoyance (seeing), and clairsentience (feeling).

When connecting with earthbound spirits, it is also important be sure our energy fields are protected. Without protecting our energy field, we expose ourselves to the energy that is keeping the spirit trapped. It becomes more difficult to determine what energy is ours and what energy is attached to the spirit.

Spirit communication comes naturally to some and can be learned by others

Chapter Twenty Seven

LISTENING TO SPIRIT SIGNALS

Before we begin communicating with spirits, we initially need to overcome our fear of them. As mentioned earlier, when we begin seeing them as a soul who is trapped in an experience, it is easier to transform our fear to compassion.

I believe the next step is to learn how to listen. Spirits are using the tools they have available to them to communicate with us and it is important that we begin listening to them.

They let us know they are with us in this dimension by several means. One of the most common is through the use of electricity. After all, spirits are energy and this is something they can manipulate. Lights flicker or radios and TVs go on and off. This isn't meant to frighten us but rather to let us know they are there.

Movement is another way. They will move a picture frame, a small article sitting on a table, or a piece of jewelry. The movie, *Ghost,* comes to mind when I think of spirits practicing how to move objects.

Scents can be another way we pick up signals. If a person was a smoker, you may smell the smoke just as if they are in the room.

The same might happen if they wore a particular perfume or fragrance.

As more and more people become clairvoyant, the spirit or spirits may come to you in a dream, as it did when the two spirits showed me they were attached to my husband. (See Chapter Three)

The next step that is very important is to trust the children in our lives. You may not be able to see or hear the spirits, but your child might. When they tell you that they see a spirit in the house or a certain room, it is important that you believe them and let them know that you are there to help. Many people call me because of a child who sees something in their home and they believe them and act on it.

This wasn't always the case. Too many adults I have met over the years did not have people around them when they were children who took them seriously. If they shared what they saw, they were told it was their imagination, and they were crazy or they were simply ignored.

When I was visiting Old Town in San Diego, I was very impressed by a dad's reaction to his son seeing a spirit and it gave me great hope to what is changing in our culture.

I was ready to walk into one of the historic buildings when a boy of about 5- years old was standing at the door with his dad. The boy told his dad that he didn't want to go in the building because a dead person was in there. I half expected the dad to dismiss his son's request but was wonderfully surprised when the dad told his son, "That's ok, we don't need to go in this building. Let's go to the next one."

The fact that the son was believed and supported by his dad will make all the difference in the world for this boy. Because he was believed, I trust that his ability to see spirits will not shut down.

Spirit communication can happen when we quiet our minds and release our fears

ATTACHMENTS

Attachments are energetic cords or bonds that can be created by the soul who is passing over or by someone they are leaving behind. There are two distinct ways that these energetic cords are created. They can be created by either the soul that is leaving or the people they are leaving behind.

Attachments created by a person or group of people the soul is leaving behind are usually emotional in nature. If the loss of life is especially tragic, it will result in strong emotional ties, which will prevent their loved one from moving on.

An attachment created by the soul passing might stem from a belief that they are responsible for a person or a group of people. Instead of moving onto their next experience, they choose to stay out of obligation.

A soul can also stay because of an attachment they have to a house or piece of land. For instance, if they have put a lot of blood, sweat and tears in creating something, they may feel a resistance to leaving it behind.

In some instances, when I am called to space clear a home and release spirits, the owner of the house will instruct me to release only the "bad" spirits and not the "good" ones, as they enjoy having them around. This is an attachment on the homeowner's part and whatever the reason for not wanting the "good" spirits to go, keeps the spirits from continuing in their soul evolution.

If a soul is ready to leave, we simply give it the opportunity to do so whether we want it to leave or not. To open a doorway and then decide who gets to leave and who stays creates karma because we are stopping the evolution of a soul.

Releasing attachments can help our loved ones pass over with ease

SOUL RETRIEVAL

The stories shared in Part One of this book are about retrieving souls. Soul retrieval is the process of finding a soul who is lost and returning them to their oversoul.

Oversoul: a term used to describe both the expansiveness of our own soul/spirit and our connection to the field of oneness.

The first few times I led a group space clearing, I was surprised to see one or more souls waiting on the other side as the souls were being helped. As they were ready and waiting to welcome them, everyone in our group who was assisting, sensed that a big celebration was taking place when they were finally returned.

An analogy would be to envision a building that collapses in an earthquake with dozens of people inside. The relatives of the trapped victims do not have the knowledge or equipment necessary to free them but are standing by, waiting for their loved ones to be rescued. Then rescuers come with equipment and begin to safely free the victims. As they are found and brought out into the light, their grateful relatives greet them with open arms and tears of joy for being returned safely.

Once the celebration calms down, the relatives then turn their attention to the lightworkers who freed them and shower them with gratitude.

This is the experience that happens every time a soul is found and returned to the group of souls waiting for them. It is wonderful to witness the celebration happening. The love and gratitude that is showered over those doing the work is nothing short of profound.

When a soul piece is stuck in an experience, all of the light this piece holds is trapped with it. During a retrieval, the lost soul is found, the energy keeping it trapped is released, and the soul then continues on its spiritual journey.

As lightworkers, we can help the soul release whatever shock, emotion or attachments are keeping the soul stuck. This varies from soul to soul and every situation is unique.

Sometimes the souls or group of souls need to forgive the person who caused the trauma or the situation that is keeping them stuck. Sometimes an emotional or mental attachment needs to be released in order for the spirit to move on.

Once the energy is cleared and the spirit is once again connected with their heart energy, I know they are ready to go home. I then open up a portal for them. This time they are able to see it clearly and as I invite them to enter, they step into it and, like a fast speed elevator, are lifted out of the third dimension to continue their soul journey.

Healing happens on many levels when we become rescuers of lost souls

Chapter Thirty

MY OWN SOUL RETRIEVAL

After I started helping others reconnect with their soul pieces, I had the opportunity to find and reconnect with one of my own.

One night, I had a clairvoyant dream where I became the observer watching the following scene play out:

I was in a house with my husband and there was a knock on the door. My husband answered it and was immediately shot. There was an instant knowing that the person who shot my husband had also killed our son. I saw myself panic and try to hide in another room. The shooter followed and shot me, too.

As I continued to watch, I saw my soul leave my body, move outside of the house and become a spirit who could not stop looking into one of the windows of the house. I felt it was stuck in a state of disbelief of what had just transpired.

I woke up from the dream and immediately went into meditation to connect with this soul piece, release it from its state of shock and return it to my oversoul.

As I reconnected with the light of this missing soul piece, I could feel my energy field expand. There was a very real sense of recognition and remembering that this soul piece was indeed a part of me. For the next days, I felt peaceful and calm with a sense of wholeness I had not experienced before.

I was grateful to have a personal soul retrieval experience. It helped me understand what others experienced during their soul retrieval sessions.

We have the opportunity to use our unique abilities to help ourselves

LAND HEALING

As we help trapped spirits move on, we are also helping the earth. The emotional energy that was created by trapping spirits in this dimension has been absorbed by the land where the event occurred.

Only when we have an understanding that like attracts like can we begin to see that a traumatic event will attract another traumatic event. The energy from all of these events continue to build, adding layer after layer of density.

This was demonstrated during one of my trips to San Diego when a couple asked me to find out what was happening outside their bedroom window. They lived close to the downtown Historic Gaslamp Quarter. Almost every Friday and Saturday night, after the restaurants and bars closed, they would become startled and awakened by a couple arguing loudly. This happened directly under their second floor bedroom window. Many of the couples would break up, thus ending the argument.

When I tuned into the area beneath their window, I saw a dark cloud of energy. Asking to see what created this cloud, I saw a scene where a couple started arguing. Then the argument ended when the man stabbed the woman. The intensity of this experience continued to attract couples that had not resolved their differences, thus creating more layers of negativity to the space.

After clearing the energy of the original argument and the negativity it attracted, there were no more arguing couples on weekends to wake up the tenants upstairs.

I believe we are in a co-creative process of healing and evolution with our planet. The earth is a living being who is experiencing her own evolution and as she evolves, she is supporting the evolution of humanity.

As humanity evolves, we are assisting with our best efforts to help the earth. This means cleaning up the mess that was created while we existed in darkness and separation. With more and more people becoming conscious, we are remembering what our soul came here to do. And for some of us, that includes transforming and uplifting the vibration of the planet.

Each time a home or a piece of land is cleared of lower vibrations, that piece of the earth can anchor the higher vibrations. It is referred to as creating Heaven on Earth by bringing fifth dimensional frequencies and anchoring them into our third dimensional world.

When we begin the important work of transforming and releasing spirits and the energy keeping them stuck, our earth becomes a more hospitable and friendly place to be.

When we heal ourselves, we heal the earth. When we heal the earth, we heal ourselves

Chapter Thirty-Two

TRANSITIONING WITH EASE

Over the years, many people have expressed to me their desire to learn how to help souls transition in the best way possible.

If we think of the passing of the soul from the body, we can compare it to a birthing. It is the soul birthing into a new experience. Much like the birthing process of a soul entering a body as a baby is being born, death is the soul leaving the body and entering a new stage of its experience.

It can be a joyful experience for the soul as it transitions into a more expanded field, unhindered by the physical form of the body. The people who are left behind are saddened, as they can no longer enjoy the physical presence of that person. And many times, the soul that has passed, tries to let their loved ones know they are doing just fine.

What we have believed in the past about death and dying is quickly changing as more people are beginning to feel, see or communicate with a soul after they pass. We are beginning to see the soul, or spirit, as something that lives on after it leaves the physical body, which is shifting our perception regarding death.

What would our society look like if we honored and supported a person in death as much as we honor and support the birth of a child? I hold a vision for our world that this will happen as more people understand this beautiful process. Actually, this is already happening.

I also have a vision that fewer souls get stuck as they pass out of their bodies. In order for this to happen, we need to learn how to clear our karma while in a physical body, release our attachments to people and places and prepare for the passing of the soul out of a body.

I was recently given the opportunity to help in the passing of a loved one as shared in the next chapter.

We are beginning to understand that death is a transition, or birthing into another experience

MY MOTHER'S STORY

During the process of writing this book, my mother was diagnosed with Alzheimer's. A few months later, on Mother's Day 2016, she fell and broke her right femur. The trauma from the fall along with being moved out of her familiar environment had accelerated her Alzheimer's.

After her rehabilitation was complete, she was moved to a memory care facility. We were told that it usually takes thirty days for people with Alzheimer's to adjust to their new surroundings but my mother never did. My parents had been married for sixty-seven years and had never been apart, so being in a place without my dad was very difficult for her.

Throughout her stay at both the rehab and memory care facilities, she would relate things that happened to her that she felt was real. One particular morning she woke up angry and crying and told the staff that three nurses came in during the night, beat her and tied her to the window. From my understanding, what she described did happen but not in this current reality. She was tapping into a past life experience and in her current state could not tell when it had occurred.

One of the tools I have gained over the years is how to release my own karma and how to help others release theirs. Knowing that my mom's karma was surfacing, and not wanting my mom to linger in a body and mind that no longer worked for her, I started helping her clear her karma.

Many times, the soul will choose to stay in body until they have cleared enough of their karma. For some, this could take years. With help, the length of time can be shortened.

After just four months in the memory care unit, she began to decline quickly and was moved to hospice care. Looking back, I feel my mom (on a soul level) arranged to get herself to a safe place to pass over. Once she entered hospice, her waking time became less and less each day. The people working at hospice were wonderful, loving souls who cared for her with gentleness and compassion. I know my mom felt it.

I arrived in Milwaukee on Sunday, January 15 and was there as my mom passed on January 16. As I came to see her the evening before she passed, I felt like I was called to be the midwife for her soul.

Having said my goodbyes and before leaving, I opened a portal for her to leave. I assured her there were guides and angels to help her pass on. Indeed, the next morning, my sister-in-law saw one of my mom's cousins who had passed a few years before in the room, waiting for her. She passed quietly and peacefully that afternoon.

Since then, she has contacted several family members in their dream states and has sent me messages to let me know she is doing great. No longer trapped in a body and mind that wasn't working for her, she is free to continue her experience as a beautiful soul of the universe.

> *Using our abilities to help a loved one transition to a new life is the greatest gift we can give*

NEXT STEP

There are several resources available to empower you to help release souls. Annette has created two packages that address both spirits attached to a person and a spirit or spirits that need releasing from the environment.

If you, a friend or family member has a spirit attached, a Personal Clearing package is available to assist you.

Personal Clearing Package Includes:

Tubes of Light Meditation
Cleansing Your Etheric Field E-Book
Large Quantum Energy Ring
Guided Personal Clearing Meditation
Quantum Energy Ring Guidebook

If there are spirits ready to be released in your home or work environment, there is a Space Clearing package available to assist you:

Space Clearing Package

Tubes of Light Meditation for Your Home
Large Quantum Energy Ring
Guided Space Clearing Meditation
Quantum Energy Ring Guidebook
Filling Your Home with Light Meditation

Work with Annette

Many opportunities are available to improve your skills, gain confidence and deepen your connection to this work. She offers:

Personal Clearing Sessions
Home, office or land Clearing Sessions
Lectures and workshops in your community
Online classes

Stay connected with Annette by going to her Join My Community section on her website.

For more information about any of the above, visit www.ReleasingLostSouls.com

RESOURCES

Diamond, Marie. *Transform Your Life,* London, England, Marie Diamond Publishing, 2018.

Cayce, Edgar. *Beyond Death.* Virginia Beach, VA, A.R.E. Press. 2008.

Cayce, Edgar. *Reincarnation and Karma.* Virginia Beach, VA, A.R.E. Press. 2005.

Hawkins, David R. *Power vs. Force.* Carlsbad, CA, Hay House, Inc. 2014.

Weiss, Brian L. *Many Lives, Many Masters.* New York, Grand Central Publishing. 1996.

Weiss, Brian L. *Same Soul, Many Bodies.* New York, Free Press. 2004.

Media Reference:

100 Years Later Oregon Remembers Worst Fire (Silver Lake, Oregon), Los Angeles Times, 1994. (Chapter 9 reference to news article)

http://articles.latimes.com/1994-12-25/local/me-12857_1_christmas-eve

Meditation

Tubes of Light Meditation https://we.tl/w6QBIg7zzF

ABOUT THE AUTHOR

Annette Rugolo is known and respected worldwide as a transformation teacher, speaker, Master Dowser and environmental healer.

Her training in healing modalities, energy healing, as well as studying and mentoring with Marie Diamond inspired her to enter the field of transformational energy work. In 2012, Annette started her company, Conscious Life Resources, with the goal of expanding her vision of bringing enlightened classes and products to people around the world. Her company currently works with worldwide distributors, and she mentors students in more than 20 countries.

Annette's passion is helping people align with their soul purpose. Her deep understanding and highly intuitive ability to connect with energy, helps to her guide clients and students to release emotional, mental and karmic patterns that hold them back from living a life of purpose. As a transformational speaker and mentor, she offers practical tools to begin their journey of change.

Annette currently resides in the Minneapolis, Minnesota with her husband, Tony. Together they have 6 children and 8 grandchildren.

Information on Annette's transformation classes, products and services available at:

www.AnnetteRugolo.com
www.ReleasingLostSouls.com